# The Northwest
## Pacific Coast and Cascades

# The Northwest
## Pacific Coast and Cascades

Photographs by Gary Braasch

Text by Bruce Brown

RIZZOLI
NEW YORK

The photographer wishes to acknowledge the publications and organizations who first published or commissioned some of the photographs which appear in this work: *Outside* Magazine, National Park Service, *Oregon Times, Oregon* Magazine, *Popular Photography, Audubon* Magazine, *Life,* Brown + Dugan Associates, Gary Albertson Design, *Washington* Magazine, Hill Design, and *Communication Arts* Magazine.

*Front cover: Head of Khutzeymateen Inlet, British Columbia*

*Back cover: Latourell Falls, Columbia River Gorge*

*Frontispiece: Monkey flower and other alpine flowers along Parnassus Creek, Garibaldi Provincial Park, British Columbia*

First published in the United States of America in 1988 by
RIZZOLI INTERNATIONAL PUBLICATIONS, INC.
597 Fifth Avenue, New York, NY 10017

Library of Congress Cataloging-in-Publication Data
Braasch, Gary.
  The Northwest : Pacific Coast and Cascades.
  Bibliography: p.
  1. Northwest, Pacific—Description and travel—
1981–    —Views. I. Brown, Bruce.    II. Title.
F852.3.B73 1988    917.95         87-43268
ISBN 0-8478-0914-5
ISBN 0-8478-0915-3 (pbk.)

Designed by Gilda Hannah
Original map by Richard O. Malin
Set in type by David E. Seham Associates, Inc., Metuchen, NJ
Printed and bound in Japan

*For Bruce who has gone ahead,*
*and Cedar who is here now*

# Preface by Gary Braasch

"There is no land, it is all mountains, forests, and water," explained the Haida guide to Newton Chittenden during his exploration of the Queen Charlotte Islands in 1884. This was the setting of Northwest Indian myths: the time long ago when there were no finite boundaries. Heaven and Earth, the living and the spirit worlds, animals and humans could transform one into the other at will. That such a time is not fully gone, that transformations still occur, is apparent to all who travel through the landscapes of Western British Columbia, Washington, and Oregon. One sets out for someplace, but enroute the mountains, forests, water, and sky unfurl and interact in staggering complexity. Each new landscape formed has a quality such that, should the traveler stop to admire it, he will be transformed in some small way before reaching his destination.

Of course, these days most of us are "too busy" to stop. The land continues to change though, and it has been my job and privilege to stop often and attempt to photograph the resulting transformation. Surely, I have been changed in the sixteen years since I arrived in Portland direct from Nebraska, Chicago, and various other places courtesy of the United States Air Force. Time after time the anonymous landscape, the unexpected vista, has wielded magic as powerful as that of the more celebrated sights of the Northwest. The resulting photographs have sometimes been so energized that they changed my outlook and altered my vision.

I don't need a photograph to remember the stormy afternoon on Mount Hood when, climbing above the meadows over fast-melting snowpack, I looked back to see the sun being reflected through a tiny break in the clouds on the Columbia River, sixty miles away. It was a magnificent instinctive lesson on the water cycle of the Cascades and the spirit of the Great River. I shot instinctively, too, automatically gauging the exposure and composition in the few seconds before the clouds extinguished the river's light. Although I don't need the picture for my memory, I have it to learn from and for others to experience the energy of that moment.

This epiphany on the mountain is one of many moments of revelation in this collection of photographs. There are also moments of simple beauty, records of the ongoing Creation both violent and incremental. The images are impressionistic, and I hope in being so they are symbolic of the nature of the Pacific Slope that we all come to love in our own time, through our own small changes, in our favorite places.

The photographs in this book are reminders of the unity of weather, natural life, and human work. From the coast to the Coast Range to the Cascades, the entire complex network is home to those of us who live here, no less than our own yard or valley is home, and no less than the whole earth is home. Just as the billions of tiny acts of life make up the sum of the area, so the sum of our individual knowledge of this place creates a network of caring that can protect the whole landscape, if we are listening to one another.

As we are transformed by the magic of the land, and as we in turn transform it, may we learn to transcend the boundaries of state and nation whenever necessary to keep the fabric whole. May we say with one voice, mindful of the Haida Indian guide: "This land is our home, it is all mountains, forests, and water—it sustains us and it is ours to protect."

# The Northwest by Bruce Brown

T he morning fog had burned off by the time we reached the far islands. We had crossed the open water of Clayoquot Sound quickly, and now we began to slow as we approached land. Near the warm, sun-baked shore of the first island, we drifted into a kelp bed and pulled our paddles. Almost immediately, the sinuous forest of seaweed stopped our kayak and anchored it in the midst of the tidal current.

It was high summer in the Northwest, with the temperature in the mid-80s and a light wind from the north. As our kayak spun lazily in the kelp, we could see back across Browning Passage to the town of Tofino, where we had launched earlier that day.

Tofino, which was named by the Spanish explorers Dionisio Galiano and Cayetano Valdes in 1792, is the largest town on Clayoquot Sound. Located at the terminus of the Marine Highway on the Pacific coast of British Columbia's Vancouver Island, Tofino is as charming an end of the road as you are ever likely to find. Every year, thousands of tourists from all over the world explore its picturesque streets and docks.

We had left all that behind, though, and ventured into the view. It was wonderfully relaxing to lie back and drift in the sun, but after a few minutes we disengaged ourselves from the kelp and paddled on, bearing north between Nelson and Morpheus islands. Here we caught the tide and accelerated. The green water boiled and boomed around us impressively, but actually posed no threat to our small boat.

That was not to say that I would want to be out on Clayoquot Sound in a vessel of any size during most of the year. The Pacific Northwest coast can be awesome in its violence. The storms that constantly spin out of the North Pacific still can swallow the best-equipped modern fishing vessels, as in the recent case of the one hundred twenty-seven-foot-long *Nordfjord*. Sometimes the sea takes its victims without a trace, but more often it deposits the detritus on remote wilderness beaches.

Although old-timers complain that the best beachcombing is all in the past, more people than ever congregate at choice spots on the coast during the winter storm season. From the deep mountainous fjords of southeast Alaska to British Columbia's oceanic islands, to the inland sea of Washington, to Oregon's classic headlands, they walk the shore—often with their backs to the wind—on the lookout for booty from the sea, especially the prized glass balls that were once commonly used as floats on Oriental fishing nets.

This was an entirely different sort of day, however. Like a bubble poised momentarily in the hand, it seemed almost dreamlike in its calmness. Then we heard the sound of an outboard motor somewhere to the west. Within a couple of minutes an inflatable Zodiac boat roared into view. We were glad to see the speeding craft, for we had been told that our destination was easy to miss. We suspected the Zodiac was headed the same place we were, and sure enough, when we rounded the next point we saw the black-and-orange boat had stopped on the forested shore of Meares Island.

By the time we had paddled across, the Zodiac had picked up a half-dozen people and had headed back the way it came. This made room for us at the "Meares dock," which was made of two logs nailed together and lashed with nylon rope to a tree on the shore. We hauled our two-man Klepper Aerius out of the water and stashed it in the Meares Island Tribal Park that the Clayoquot Indians unofficially established in 1984 to stress their claim to their ancestral homeland. To raise money for the battle to save Meares, and spread word of the island's special beauty, the Friends of Clayoquot Sound run charters to the island, which for a modest fee will take you out in a Zodiac and then come back and get you several hours later.

There were a half-dozen people from such an excursion sitting on the shore waiting for the next Zodiac run when we pulled in. One woman in khaki walking shorts said they had hiked the loop trail that swings in a several-mile arc around the Arakun Flats peninsula at the base of Meares' Mount Colnett, which is named for an early English sea captain and trader. Many of the island's largest trees are found here. I asked the woman if they had seen any impressive specimens, and she nodded. She said they had decided to measure one old giant, and found it took nine of them stretched arm to arm to reach around the tree at the base. "It was nine hugs wide," she concluded with a smile.

It took a few seconds for our eyes to adjust to the dusky light of the deep woods, but soon we could see immense trees standing all around. Beneath them, the underbrush stood as tall as many conventional trees, and skunk cabbage grew the size of Saint Bernards. This was the old-growth forest that once covered the entire Northwest. The western red cedar, Sitka spruce, western hemlock, and Douglas fir have never been logged here, allowing them to attain full maturity. Many are more than fifteen hundred years old and one hundred and fifty feet tall. An ancient known locally as the Hanging Garden Tree is believed to be Canada's largest western red cedar. Located on the banks of nearby Meares Creek, this giant has a girth of sixty-one feet.

Following the narrow path through the forest, it was easy to imagine the island two hundred years ago when the first white men set foot on this coast. Meares Island is named for British sea captain John Meares, who built the first white habitation on the Northwest Coast at Nootka Sound in 1788. A free-booting merchant who was operating in violation of the British East India Company's monopoly on trade with the Far East, Meares claimed he purchased from the Indians a considerable portion of Nootka Sound, along with the next inlet forty miles to the south, Clayoquot Sound. The English and Spanish both bought sea otter pelts from the Clayoquot Indians, but the first white man to actually live for a time on the sound was the American Captain Robert Gray.

Returning to the Northwest in June 1791 after becoming the first American to circumnavigate the globe, Gray decided to winter at Adventure Cove on Meares Island, across from the Indian village of Opitsaht. Gray had met the Clayoquot chief Wickananish on his previous voyage, and the two enjoyed very cordial relations. On Christmas, Gray gave a dinner party for the Indians aboard his ship, the *Columbia,* and on New Year's Eve, he and his crew joined the Indians for a roaring party at Opitsaht. By late winter, Gray had nearly finished building a second ship, the forty-five-ton *Adventure,* and purchased all the available sea otter pelts in the Clayoquot area.

*Pages 10–11: Mount Hood and the Hood River Valley, Oregon*

Then just as they were about to depart, the Americans learned of an apparent Indian plot against them. No attack actually occurred, but as Gray sailed out of Clayoquot Sound on February 23, 1792, he ordered the destruction of the Indian village where he had so recently been entertained. The young officer assigned to the task, John Bolt, noted sadly:

> I am grieved to think that Captain Gray would let his passions go so far. This village was about half a mile in diameter, and contained upwards of 200 houses, generally well built . . . Every door that you entered was in resemblance to an human head and beast's head, the passage being through the mouth, besides which there was much more rude carved work about the dwellings, some of which was by no means inelegant. This fine village, the work of ages, was in short time totally destroyed.[1]

A few days later, the Clayoquot Indians returned to rebuild Opitsaht. White explorers and adventurers continued to visit the area sporadically, but for the next century the Indians had Meares Island and the waters around it to themselves. They were initially untouched by both the Northwest boundary treaty between England and the United States and the confederation of Canada. Finally in 1874, two years after Canada became a nation, the first permanent white settlement was established on Clayoquot Sound.

The insidious effects of alcohol and Christian missionaries had already weakened Indian culture, and now the traditional Indian ways came under direct attack from another quarter. In 1884 the Canadian government outlawed the potlatch, which literally meant "giving" and was the central winter ceremony of all Northwest Coast Indians, including the Clayoquot. This made it a crime to participate in the storied rites which were intimately associated with the great carvings that have subsequently earned the Northwest Coast Indian artists world recognition. To assure that Indian children did not learn their rich heritage, they were taken from their homes and sent to specially built boarding schools like Christi, the Catholic school on Meares.

Canadian treatment of Northwest Indians during this period resembled that afforded Indians in the United States, except that it was even harsher. Whereas the United States generally purchased the Indian land within its borders by treaty, the Canadian government appropriated Indian land by parliamentary edict. Although the Clayoquot Indians had never relinquished the deed to their ancestral homes, the Canadian government began virtually giving the land away to white settlers in 1905. Homesteaders were eligible for one hundred and sixty acres of land; meanwhile, timber speculators were allowed to preempt thousands of acres of incredibly rich forest, including a portion of Meares. When the Native Reserves were first laid out in 1908, the Indians of Clayoquot and elsewhere in British Columbia received about seven acres a person.

Despite all this, life for the Clayoquot remained relatively unchanged well into the twentieth century. The Indians still lived in their traditional villages, such as Opitsaht, and they still relied on the same basic resources, like salmon, for their livelihood. According to a Clayoquot leader, as late as the 1950s the sockeye salmon runs into the Kennedy River at the head of Clayoquot Sound were strong enough to support about thirty Indian seine boats, each with a crew of five. Things began to change after 1956, however. That year the first dirt road was built connecting Tofino with

the outside world, and more Clayoquot Sound forests were awarded to the timber industry, including many of the picturesque little islands around Meares.

Logging had not yet reached Tofino or Meares, but its effects were evident in the decline in the Kennedy River salmon runs that were devastated by the thoughtless and wasteful forest practices. Whole mountainsides were clearcut and left to erode, choking the streams with muddy debris. By the early 1970s, the Indian salmon fishing industry had been completely wiped out, and the canneries that were once so prominent a part of the Tofino waterfront closed. As fishing declined, tourism emerged as the mainstay of the local economy. The fabulous setting of this forest archipelago—together with its reliable whale watching—began to draw people from all over the world, especially after the opening of nearby Pacific Rim Park in 1971.

Then in 1983, the British Columbia Provincial government gave timber companies, which claimed timber rights to much of Meares Island under grants from 1905, approval to log ninety percent of the island. When the first Macmillan Bloedel loggers stepped off the *Kennedy Queen* onto Meares, however, they were met by a crowd of local people who welcomed them to Meares but warned them to leave their chainsaws in the boat. Shortly afterwards, the Clayoquot Indians won an injunction barring any logging on Meares until the court could address the deeper issues of land ownership and aboriginal rights raised by the Clayoquot.

That court case, which is currently under way, will determine whether this forest will survive as it has for thousands of years, or only in the memory of books like this. The battle over Meares has many wider ramifications, as well. It is being watched closely by many groups—by members of the timber industry and environmentalists, by Canadians and Americans, by Indians and non-Indians—as an important part of the ongoing struggle for control of the Northwest landscape.

Such conflicts underscore the fact that the story of the Northwest is an unfinished one. Socially, politically, even geologically—as the eruption of Mount St. Helens demonstrates—the region is still changing and coming into being. Or perhaps it is more accurate to say that the Northwest is shaped by forces in oscillation, with its personality perpetually in movement within constantly recognizable bounds.

It is typical of the Northwest that the land—not the people—should provide the central character. Despite its increasing urbanization and sophistication, the Northwest remains a place where people assume the environment is important. Perhaps the reason the Northwest landscape looms so large in the minds of its residents is that it provides much more than horizon line. Here is North America's most extensive archipelago, its greatest tributaries to the Pacific, and its most active volcanic mountain range.

Back in the kayak as we continued our journey, we saw thousands of shore birds winging to the north toward Opitsaht and Adventure Cove. The birds were flying in unison, turning first left and then right. Light on one side and dark on the other, they seemed to appear and vanish like venetian blinds.

Although we altered our course, we still had to fight the current more than on the way out. The late afternoon sun was directly in our faces, and I noticed I was beginning to drip sweat off the end of my nose.

*Page 17: Goat Rocks Wilderness, Washington*

The wind tapered off to an occasional wandering zephyr, and then vanished altogether.

Off the point of Morpheus, an immature bald eagle flew so low over us that we could hear his labored flight. Trying to land in a spruce top along the shore, he nearly lost his perch as the branch shook wildly under his weight. When we turned around, a memorable scene awaited in the channel to the west. Against the dark, shaggy shoreline of the opposite island a huge curtain of gauzy steam hung in the still air. Suffused with the warm rays of the late afternoon sun, it shone like diaphanous silk.

This was the spout of a whale that was traveling with us down the channel. It was probably a gray whale of the sort that draws thousands of people to the commercial whale tours in Tofino every year. The tours concentrate on an area of the Pacific off Flores Island, where the animals congregate to feed on relatively shallow mud banks.

There it is common to see these whales on the surface, catching their breath for the next dive and staining the water brown with the muck they expel after straining it for the tiny creatures that provide their food. When they have refreshed themselves, they dive with the characteristic fluke-high farewell of their kind.

The cold grip of the river on my legs always startled me, no matter how much I prepared for it. Even through hip boots I could feel it tightening as I waded across the knee-deep riffle. Reaching the other side, I paused in the luminescent shade of a maple grove to take my bearings.

A thistledown ball rolled by on the surface of the river, while overhead a flycatcher gorged itself on insects that it took at the apogee of its roller-coaster flight. Bright fall colors splashed the forested ridges on either side of the valley, and the spires of the Cascade Mountains loomed behind, glittering with the snow fields that fed the current I had just crossed.

Although many of the people I met on the river mistook me for a fisherman, I was actually not interested in catching fish, or even counting them very systematically. My purpose was simply the pleasure of being present for one of nature's great migratory miracles. Somewhere in the green waters around me were Chinook salmon that had been born here years before, migrated to the sea, and now returned home to spawn and die.

The river was the Yakima. Icy, exuberant, and absolutely pellucid in its upper reaches, the Yakima drains a sizeable portion of the middle Cascades in Washington state. After rushing through two spectacular canyons in its upper eighty miles, the river flows out into a broad lower valley near the city of Yakima and meanders more than one hundred miles to its confluence with the Columbia River near Hanford, Washington.

With a mainstem length of 1,234 miles, the Columbia is the largest North American affluent of the Pacific. It drains most of the Cascade Mountains and northern Rockies, including parts of five American states and one Canadian province. Only the Mississippi in the United States is larger, and even it can not boast either the vertical fall or tremendous

*Pages 18–19: Lake Ingalls, Alpine Lakes Wilderness, Washington*

scenic variety of the Columbia as it courses from mountain summit to the sea. Yet for all its majesty, the Columbia is not the Pacific Northwest's only great river. In fact, one of the features that distinguishes the Northwest is the fact that it contains two of the world's major rivers.

Barely three hundred miles north of the Columbia bar, the Fraser River debouches into the Pacific near Vancouver, British Columbia. Second only to the Columbia among North American affluents of the Pacific, the Fraser follows a course parallel to the Columbia, and actually comes within a few miles of the other river in British Columbia's Cariboo Mountains. Although distinct in character and history, the two great rivers share a certain resemblance. In fact, early Canadian fur trader Simon Fraser mistakenly believed he was on the Columbia for almost all of his exploration of the river that bears his name. Today, the two rivers divide the region into approximate thirds. Just as the Columbia separates Washington and Oregon, the Fraser, which flows within a dozen miles of the United States and Canada border, effectively separates Washington and British Columbia.

Rivers also mark the edges of the Northwest. In the extreme northern portion of British Columbia, the line is the wild, cold Stikine River, which flows down to the Pacific just north of Wrangell, Alaska. Approximately two thousand miles to the south, the regional boundary is the picturesque Klamath River, which flows through stately redwood groves to the Pacific at Klamath, California. In between the Stikine and the Klamath are hundreds of significant, independent river systems, including the Nass and Skeena in British Columbia; the Skagit, Quillayute, and Chehalis in Washington; and the Umpqua and Rogue in Oregon. Although little known outside the region, they dwarf many East Coast rivers. The Stikine, for instance, is nearly one-third larger than the Hudson, and the Klamath could swallow a dozen rivers the size of the Concord.

It was on these myriad Northwest rivers that the native American people built their rich culture. From the primeval forest along its banks they took the cedar for their renowned carvings. Following the cycle of natural provender, they named their months after the food that nature provided at that time. For virtually all these tribes, the most important season was "the time of heavy salmon spawning." All along the Northwest Coast (and in fact across the Pacific on the northeast coast of Asia as well) the native peoples practiced the First Salmon Ceremony in recognition of these fishes' vital importance. After that spring's first fish was ceremonially prepared and eaten, the bones were solemnly returned to the water. The Indians believed the salmon runs would cease if people did not observe the correct rituals and act ethically.

We will never know the exact magnitude of the wild salmon runs before the coming of the white man, but the first explorers made it clear that they were one of the natural wonders of the region. In fact, it was a piece of salmon, eaten on the Lemhi River in the mountains of what is now Idaho, which first told Meriwether Lewis that the Lewis and Clark Expedition had crossed the continental divide and was "on the waters of the Pacific." Later, during the summer of 1805, as Lewis and Clark passed down the lower Columbia River, they reported that "the multitudes of fish are almost inconceivable."[2] A half century later, in 1860, another noted traveler called the Indian fishery at Kettle Falls on the mainstem Columbia "the most wonderful I ever saw. The salmon arrive at the foot of the falls in great numbers and proceed to leap them; all day long you see one continual stream of fish in the air. . . ."[3]

*Pages 22–23: The Columbia River dividing Portland, Oregon, and Vancouver, Washington*

As Canadian and American settlement accelerated in the Northwest, the region's rivers continued to play a prominent role as sources of transportation and channels of development. Trading posts and forts were commonly located near the mouths of major rivers, and the early efforts at farming took place on the rich river-bottom soils. The rivers also gave white pioneers their principal cash crop: the lush beaver pelts that were so prized in the Chinese Imperial court. Many hogsheads of salmon were salted by the pioneers for their own provision, but it was not until the later part of the nineteenth century that canning technology made it feasible to commercially exploit the Columbia salmon runs. By the 1880s, the commercial salmon fishery on the Columbia was the greatest in the world.

In those halcyon days, all of the five species of Pacific salmon (Chinook, coho, sockeye, pink, and chum), in addition to sea-run trout and char (steelhead, cutthroat, and Dolly Varden) ran into the Columbia every month of the year. Amid this overwhelming bounty, the choicest fish were the summer Chinook, known locally as June hogs. Commonly weighing forty or more pounds and possessing the finest salmon flesh in the river, these fish were specially adapted to run up the river more than a thousand miles to spawning grounds in British Columbia. In the early days, Columbia River fishermen fished almost exclusively for June hogs, taking more than forty million pounds of the fish twice during the 1880s. The summer Chinook declined thereafter, but total catches remained high as fishermen targeted other segments of the great Columbia runs, such as the spring Chinook of the upper Yakima.

In the first volume of his autobiography, William O. Douglas recounted the dramatic impression these fish made on him as a boy growing up in Yakima. During World War I, Douglas began hiking and riding in the Cascade mountains to strengthen his polio-weakened legs. On the Tieton River, a wild headwater tributary of the Yakima, he met a Yakima Indian who taught him how to spear spring Chinook in the Indian manner. Douglas recalls the first time he stalked a big spotted-backed Chinook:

> I drove the spear down with all my strength—and lunged right into the water. In those days, I could not yet swim, and my legs went rigid with fear. . . . Luckily, I caught hold of some willows and pulled myself to shore, shivering and shaking. I looked across the river. My Indian friend was there, doubled up with laughter.[4]

There are no spring Chinook in the Tieton River today, and no June hogs in the Columbia. Both of these choice runs were exterminated during the last sixty years by United States Bureau of Reclamation dams. The Tieton Chinook that young Douglas loved were killed in 1925 by an irrigation dam which blocked the fishes' passage to their spawning grounds. Then in 1933 at a place known as Grand Coulee, the Bureau of Reclamation began erecting the largest dam in the world on the mainstem Columbia a few miles downstream from Kettle Falls. The dam Woody Guthrie called "the mightiest thing ever built by man" lacked any fish passage facilities or other provisions for the great Columbia salmon runs, and so also stands as the single most destructive action toward salmon in human history.[5]

The federal government hoped that salmon hatcheries would be able to replicate the lost upriver runs. Four hatcheries were built to mitigate the damage done by Grand Coulee, but all failed, and the June hogs

*Page 25: The Pumice Plain, five miles from the crater of Mount St. Helens, Washington*

became extinct. The same story was repeated again and again after World War II as dams were built along virtually the entire length of the Columbia and all its major tributaries. During the 1940s, the Columbia salmon catch averaged around twenty million pounds a year. By the mid-1970s, the commercial salmon catch from the Columbia had fallen to around five million pounds annually and included no summer or spring Chinook. The distress had become so general by 1978 that the federal government began considering all upriver species for inclusion on the threatened or endangered species lists.

In contrast to their cousins on the Columbia River, the salmon of the Fraser River have fared relatively well. Many runs were exterminated here too, but because the mainstem Fraser has never been dammed and hatcheries never heavily utilized, the wild fish have been able to hold their own. In fact, although the river's total salmon population has declined, it remains strong enough to make the Fraser the dominant salmon river in the Northwest today. You can still see some of the old salmon glory on the Fraser in places like the Adams River, where hundreds of thousands of flame-red fish jam the waters bank to bank during spawning season. Perhaps even more amazing are the thousands of tourists from all over the world who line the shores of the river to watch the show.

Inspired in part by scenes like those on the Adams River, pressure has grown in recent years to rebuild some of the lost Columbia River salmon runs. Following Congress' passage of the Northwest Power Act of 1980, the newly created Pacific Northwest Power Planning Council formulated a plan to selectively reintroduce salmon to areas where they have been killed off. The river chosen to showcase the rebuilding effort was the Yakima. During the mid-1980s, the federal government spent more than thirty million dollars on the Yakima to build fish ladders, screens, and other modifications to existing dams designed to help the surviving salmon.

Despite continued governmental efforts in the opposite direction—such as the current United States Army Corps of Engineers' proposal to divert the Columbia from its last free-flowing section near the confluence of the Yakima, and the recent discovery of radioactive pollution entering this same stretch of the Columbia from the United States Department of Energy's Hanford Nuclear Reservation—for the first time a serious effort is being made to rebuild the fish population that was the greatest natural marvel of the region a century ago.

I was up to my knees in the Yakima that hot afternoon to see the effects of this effort to return the wild salmon of the Columbia. Even though the laddering of Easton Dam immediately upriver was not scheduled to be completed until the next year, many of the downriver salmon restoration projects were already in place, and the fisheries' biologists were abuzz with the improvements already evident in the runs in the Yakima. Wading further upriver toward a deep pool with the color and luster of Ming jade, I quickly understood why. In the next one hundred yards I counted nearly a hundred live spring Chinook, together with twenty-five or so bleached, partly eaten salmon carcasses dotting the banks like strange, river-strewn blossoms.

Most of the salmon spawning seemed to stop at the bend in the river where you can first see the face of Easton Dam looming in the gorge, but I continued on, curious how far the salmon's urge to climb would take them. At the turn of the century, springers (along with coho and the now extinct Yakima sockeye) fought their way another fifteen or twenty miles further into the eastern Cascade Mountains. For the last fifty years ineffectively laddered Easton Dam has blocked fish passage into the headwaters of the Yakima, but that summer the dam was having a new ladder and revolving screens installed as part of the Yakima salmon restoration project.

I was just about to turn back when I came upon them. In the shadow of an overhanging grove of flame red sumac, the current had cut the bank and spilled the gravel in a raised fan. A Yakima spring Chinook female had chosen this shaded nook for the uppermost nest on the river. Here five springers, characteristically golden-green and heavily spotted, held their position with strokes so casual they almost seemed to take their motion from the current.

A handsome eight-pound female rolled on her side and began working on her nest with a pulsating flash of silver that sent a plume of silt drifting on the current. In a week she would be spawned out, and in two weeks dead, but by the time her progeny return from the Pacific, Easton Dam will be laddered and they can run up twelve miles closer to Snoqualmie Pass. And so it seems that the annual Columbia salmon spawning ritual still marks a beginning as well as an end.

It was the moment I had been waiting for. Below me to the east, the chair lift operator was skiing down from the hut, his elegant turns paralleling the now closed and silent lift. All the zippy downhill skiers had departed, and I was the last person on the upper flanks of Oregon's Mount Hood as the spring sun set into the blue distance over the Pacific.

Standing at timberline on permanent snow fields, I could see glacier-whitened volcanic cones marching south toward California. First Mount Jefferson, then Three Fingered Jack and the North, Middle, and South Sisters massifs. On and on the volcanoes went, each with a craggy face turned toward the last rays of the sun. To the north, on the other side of Mount Hood and the Columbia River, the sentinel line continued with Mount St. Helens, Mount Adams, Mount Rainier, and Mount Baker.

Free of the chair lifts because I was on cross-country skis, I continued upward in the tender light. Melt water had stopped dripping off the few remaining trees, and in the shadows the sloppy corn snow was beginning to harden into ice. I could tell the temperature was dropping rapidly, but the rhythmic kick of my skis kept me warm. I unzipped my jacket and marveled at the mountain stillness. There was absolutely no wind at all, and no sound discernable in the immense landscape except my own breathing.

Mount Hood, which loomed over a vertical mile above me into the alpenglow, is Oregon's tallest mountain at 11,235 feet. The regent of the middle Cascades, Mount Hood dominates the skyline around Portland, Oregon, the way Mount Rainier dominates around Seattle, Washington, and Mount Baker dominates east of Vancouver. Perhaps the best reflection of these volcanoes' stature is the fact that in their own domains, they are often simply referred to as "the Mountain."

Not too long ago in geologic terms, there was another giant volcano

in the chain. Located in the southern Oregon Cascades, Mount Mazama stood at least 12,000 feet high. Its multiple summits revealed a complex history of eruptions, but these were only the prelude to the dramatic finale. About six thousand years ago, Mazama collapsed on itself and then exploded into an immense pyroclastic cloud. This geological drop-kick produced one of the largest volcanic blasts known in the history of the earth.

Exceeding both the explosions of Krakatau and Katmai in terms of volume of material expelled, the destruction of Mount Mazama blanketed more than three hundred fifty thousand square miles of what is now Nevada, Idaho, Montana, Oregon, Washington, British Columbia, and Alberta with ash, some of it ten feet thick. When the smoke cleared, the lower slopes of Mazama still rose smoothly to almost 9,000 feet, but then they fell away into a huge volcanic basin, or caldera. Six miles across and a mile deep, the hole gradually filled with water, in time becoming Crater Lake, the deepest lake in the United States.

Many eruptions have rocked the Cascades since, including an explosion five thousand years ago which cost Mount Rainier 2,000 feet off its summit, and what one nineteenth-century account described as "jets of flame" on Mount Hood.[6] The most recent evidence that the Cascades have not lost their volcanic punch came on a spring morning in 1980, when Mount St. Helens erupted with a force five hundred times that of the atomic bomb that fell on Hiroshima. For Northwesterners, this is a moment frozen in time, like the assassination of John F. Kennedy and the Apollo moon landing. People remember where they were at 8:32 A.M. on May 18, 1980. I distinctly recall the boom two hundred miles away at my home in the Fraser Valley, where it was loud enough to violently rattle glass.

Geologists believe the power that drives Cascade volcanoes like Mount St. Helens is the tremendous heat at the earth's core. As the earth's hard surface plates shift with the movements of convection currents in the molten liquid mantle below, collisions and points of stress frequently occur. When the edge of one surface plate slides far enough under the edge of another, classic volcanic cones erupt to the surface above, venting superheated gasses and molten material. Newborn stratovolcanoes tend to have the classic cone shape associated with Mount Fuji, but from their first winter they are reworked by ice and snow. During the last Ice Age less than ten thousand years ago, the glaciers built up so heavily in the Cascades that they spread out and covered the lowlands as much as a mile deep between Vancouver and Salem, Oregon.

This is truly a realm of fire and ice, where creation and destruction walk hand in hand and often wear each other's garb. The 1980 eruption of Mount St. Helens killed virtually everything in a one hundred and fifty square mile area, but within weeks of the blast scientists found primitive bacteria extremely plentiful in the hot water vents and fumaroles around the blasted crater. These bacteria are believed to be among the most ancient on earth, and raise the possibility that the earth's vulcanism may have helped spread the miracle we call life in its earliest stages.

The Indians believed the mountains were gods and explained their eruptions as colossal displays of love and hate. Today, our explanations are much different, but some of the awe remains. For many Northwesterners, newcomers and natives alike, the dramatic cones crystalize the Northwest's unusual scenic beauty and stand as a constant reminder of the tremendous natural power that still animates the landscape.

*Page 31: Crab boat on Khutzeymateen Inlet, British Columbia*

When I finally stopped that evening on Mount Hood, I was far above timberline. All around, I surveyed what might be called the heart of the Cascades, since the range was named by pioneer English botanist David Douglas for the exuberant rivers that drain the area around Mount Hood.

It was also in the Cascades that Douglas saw the fir that bears his name and collected the first specimens of numerous species, including the sugar pine, largest of the world's one hundred species of pine. After months of eager anticipation, Douglas found himself in a grove of ancient sugar pine near the site of present-day Roseburg, Oregon, at noon on October 25, 1826. Unable to reach the cones suspended one hundred fifty feet in the air, Douglas began shooting his rifle to knock one down. While he was engaged in this effort, a group of not too friendly Indians surrounded him.

At first Douglas, who was alone, tried embarrassedly to explain what he knew must seem like utterly irrational behavior to the painted warriors. Soon, however, he began to fear for his life and was forced to pull a gun on the Indians. Douglas ultimately managed to elude the natives by offering to pay them for cones from the sugar pine and sending them off to seek them on the forest floor. As soon as the warriors were out of sight, the intrepid specimen collector for the Royal Horticultural Society of England hurried in the opposite direction.

The noted naturalist and wilderness advocate John Muir, who tramped Oregon's mountains during the later part of the nineteenth century, found them more peaceful, but no less inspiring. Like Douglas more than a half century before, Muir was impressed with the Cascade rivers, speaking of them "chanting altogether in one great anthem." Muir's response to the Cascade Mountains was as direct and emotional as any tourist, but he also anticipated the theories of modern geology when he observed, "Oregon as it is today is a very young country, though most of it seems old."[7]

Many have followed in the footsteps of Muir and Douglas and drawn from the land the same sense of wild solace. This is possible largely because many important portions of the Cascades remain protected, from Manning Provincial Park in British Columbia to Crater Lake National Park in Oregon. In fact, as a result of the relentless lobbying of Northwest environmentalists, the Cascades were one of the few areas of the United States to receive substantial additional wilderness protection during the administration of President Ronald Reagan.

The recent success of the Washington and Oregon wilderness acts testifies to the grass roots strength of environmentalism in the Northwest, where running rivers in rubber rafts is as important for politicians as kissing a baby is elsewhere. While not everyone agrees with the activism of the British Columbia-born organization Greenpeace, Northwesterners tend to structure their lives in a manner that allows them to enjoy the place they live. Most people may never get more involved than enjoying the sunset on the mountain, but there are inevitably some who take the Cascades as a personal challenge.

In fact, almost as soon as the white settlers arrived in the Northwest there were efforts to climb and explore the higher peaks of the Cascades. The first ascent of the tallest peak in the range, 14,410-foot Mt. Rainier, occurred in 1854 when three unknown climbers ascended from the Yakima side with the help of an Indian guide. The first confirmed ascent was in 1870, when Hazard Stevens and Philemon Van Trump were saved from freezing by a steam cave on the summit where they spent the night warmed by "Pluto's fires."[8]

The first woman to attain the summit of Mount Rainier was Faye Fuller, who accomplished the feat in 1890 and was the harbinger of the thousands of recreationalists who annually throng the slopes of all the major Cascade peaks every year for every conceivable form of recreation. Mountain climbers, backpackers, skiers, hunters, snowmobilers, picnickers, fly fishermen, dirt bikers, bird-watchers, hang gliders, and Indian shamans all share—albeit somewhat uncomfortably at times—the mountains these days.

As I watched, night welled up out of the valleys around Mount Hood, deepening and darkening as it rose. Far below, I saw the twinkling lights of cars on the highway and the gilt windows of Timberline Lodge. Shoving off with a double-pole kick, I started down. The smooth, almost mogulless terrain allowed me to develop a rhythm, and suddenly I found myself skiing in the fall line again. I let my skis run when I came to the long schuss below the last steep pitch on the Magic Mile run.

Clattering a bit on the increasingly icy snow, I skated easily around the last bend and swung to a stop in the brightly lit parking lot. Above the snow-laden roof of Timberline Lodge, I could barely make out the silhouette of Mount Hood. It was drained of all color and had become pure form.

NOTES

1. Derek Pethick, *The Nootka Connection: Europe and the Northwest Coast* (Seattle, WA: University of Washington Press, 1980), p. 113.

2. Meriwether Lewis and William Clark, *The History of the Lewis and Clark Expedition* (New York: Harper & Sons, 1893), p. 493.

3. George F.G. Stanley, ed., *Mapping the Frontier: The Frontier Diaries of Charles Wilson During the Survey of the 49th Parallel, 1858–1862, While Secretary of the British Boundary Commission* (Seattle, WA: University of Washington Press, 1970), p. 114.

4. William O. Douglas, *Go East Young Man* (New York: Random House, 1974), p. 72.

5. Bruce Brown, *Mountain in the Clouds: A Search for the Wild Salmon* (New York: Simon & Schuster, 1982), p. 85.

6. Joel Connelly, "The Unpredictable NW Volcanos," *Seattle Post-Intelligencer*, March 27, 1983, p. 17C.

7. Gideon Bosker and Jonathan Nichols, *Greetings from Oregon* (Portland, OR: Graphic Arts Center Publishing, 1987), p. 20.

8. Paul Schullery, ed., *Island in the Sky: Pioneering Accounts of Mt. Rainier, 1833–1894* (Seattle, WA: Mountaineers Books, 1987), pp. 24–78.

*Pages 34–35: Yarrow and grasses at Cascade Head Preserve, Oregon*

*Pages 36–37: Old-growth forests and Mount Hood, Columbia River Gorge*

*Page 38: Crevasse on Humes Glacier, Mount Olympus, Washington*

*Page 39: The Punchbowl, Eagle Creek, Columbia River Gorge*

Pages 40–41: *North Falls, Silver Creek State Park, Oregon*

Pages 42–43: *Seine fishing boats at Port McNeill, British Columbia*

*Page 44: Spruces and hemlock, Hoh Valley, Olympic National Park, Washington*

*Page 45: Ancient spruce forest, Khutzeymateen Inlet, British Columbia*

*Pages 46–47: School day begins, Willamette Valley, Oregon*

*Pages 56–57: Astoria, Oregon, founded in 1811 as a base for fur traders*

*Page 58: Mount Jefferson, Oregon*

*Page 59: Columbia River Gorge*

*Pages 60–61: Arch Rock Point, southern Oregon coast*

*Pages 62–63: Below the crater of Mount St. Helens*

*Page 64: Oaks and a single madrone tree, Illinois River,
Kalmiopsis Wilderness, Oregon*

*Page 65: Native fisherman, Alert Bay, British Columbia*

*Pages 66–67: Wizard Island and Crater Lake National Park,
Oregon*

*Pages 68–69: Seal Rocks, Oregon*

Page 70: Modern bear pole and house, 'Ksan Indian Village,
center of the preservation of Gitksan arts, British Columbia

Page 71: Original Haida mortuary pole, Skedans village site,
Queen Charlotte Islands

Pages 72–73: Children on the beach, Manzanita, Oregon

Pages 74–75: The Space Needle, built for the 1962 World's
Fair, a symbol of Seattle

Pages 76–77: A community built on pilings, Telegraph Cove,
British Columbia

*Page 78: St. Mary's, a historic wood frame church on the Columbia River, near Ilwaco, Washington*

*Page 79: Ramona Falls on the Pacific Crest Trail, Mount Hood*

*Pages 80–81: Pear orchard in winter*

*Pages 82–83: Painted rock dating from prehistory, Port John near Bella Bella, British Columbia*

*Page 84: Woodpecker and eagle on Tsimshian pole from Kitwancool, a replica at the British Columbia Provincial Museum, Victoria*

*Page 85: Kwagiutl Thunderbird poles and cemetery, Alert Bay, British Columbia*

*Pages 86–87: Neah-Kah-Nie Mountain, Oregon*

*Pages 88–89: Skagit Valley bulb industry, Washington*

*Page 90: Sunset, Manzanita, Oregon*

*Page 91: Moored boats on Telegraph Cove, British Columbia*

*Pages 92–93: Port Orford, Oregon*

*Pages 94–95: Setting sun reflects from Columbia River, Mount Hood, Oregon*

*Page 97: Great dunes between Florence and Coos Bay, Oregon*

*Pages 98–99: Countryside, Sheridan, Oregon*

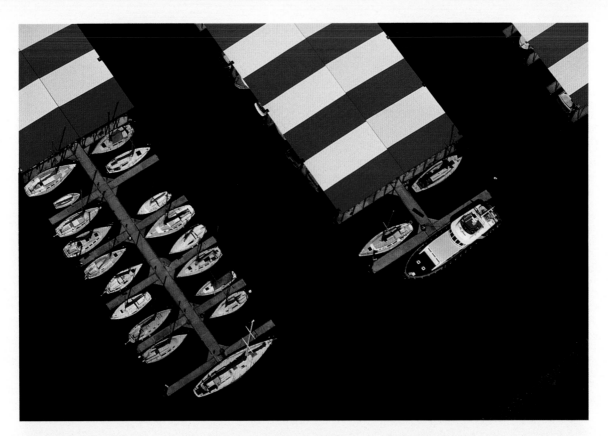

*Page 108: Khutzeymateen Valley, British Columbia*

*Page 109: Lodgepole pines and mountain hemlocks, Three Sisters, Oregon*

*Pages 110–111: Cape Perpetua, Oregon*

*Pages 112–113: Sedges along Sagar Lake, British Columbia*

*Page 114: Lava-born boulders, Cape Falcon, Oregon*
*Page 115: Pacific Ocean and mouth of Nehalem River, Oregon*

Page 116: Petroglyphs, once a common form of expression for Northwest Indians, Thorsen Creek, British Columbia

Page 117: Rivulets, Coast Range

Pages 118–119: Octopus Islands Marine Park, British Columbia

Pages 120–121: Spirit Lake and hillsides of Mount St. Helens

Pages 122–123: Lava flows, Crown Point, Columbia River Gorge

Page 124: Troller, Newport harbor

Page 125: Madrone, or Arbutus, trees, Orcas Island, Washington

*Pages 126–127: Grasses of South Slough estuary, Oregon*

*Pages 128–129: Codville Lagoon, near Bella Bella, British Columbia*

*Page 130: Storm waves at the foot of Neah-Kah-Nie Mountain*
*Page 131: Ochre stars and seaweeds, Ecola State Park, Oregon*
*Pages 132–133: Sandpipers*
*Pages 134–135: Red clover*

131

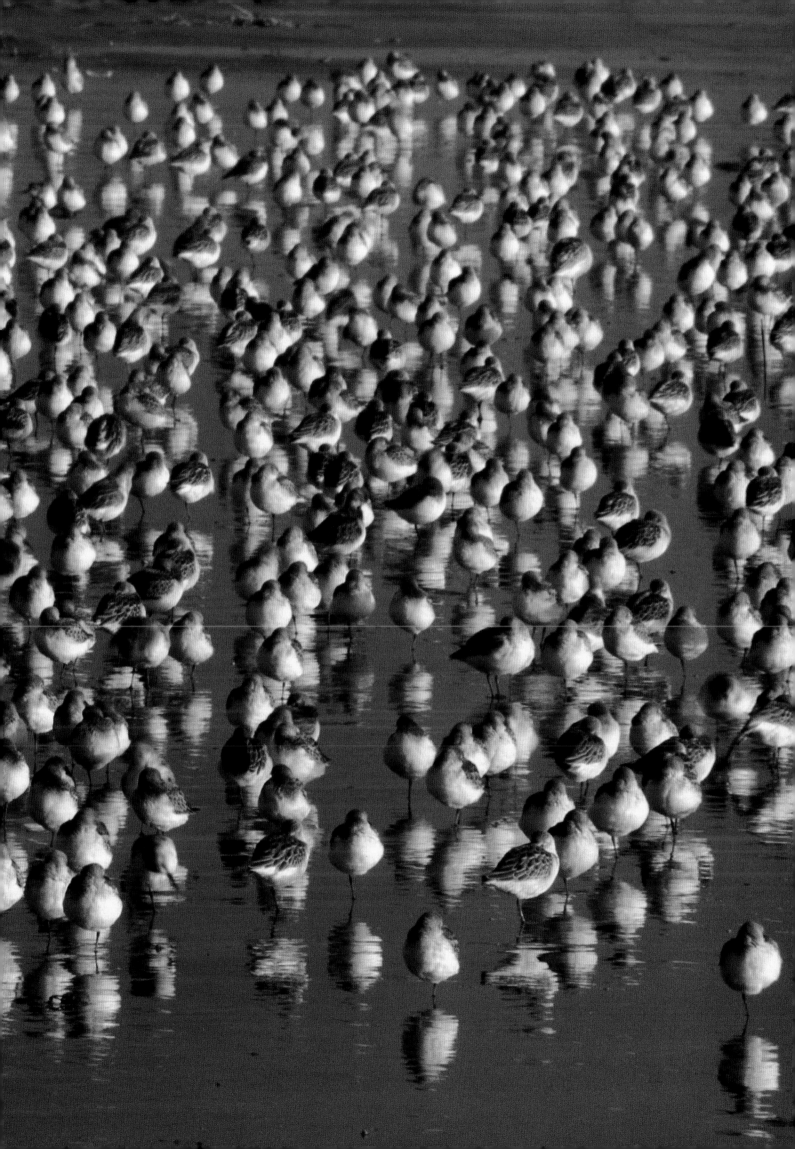

*Page 146: The Yaquina Head lighthouse near Newport, Oregon*
*Page 147: Canoeist on the Deschutes River, Oregon*

Pages 148–149: *Fisherman on outer Seal Rocks, Oregon*

Pages 150–151: *Pumice canyons on Mount Hood*

Pages 152–153: *Cream Lake Basin, Olympic National Park, Washington*

Page 154: Indian paintbrush and mountain hemlock trees,
Cascade Range

Page 155: Farmworker and tulips, Mount Vernon, Washington

Pages 156–157: Elk, Mount St. Helens

Pages 158–159: Blackfish Sound, Vancouver, Island

Pages 160–161: *Slopes of Meares Island and town of Tofino beyond, Vancouver Island*

Page 162: *Pacific Rim National Park, Vancouver Island*

Page 163: *Rogue River, Oregon*

Pages 164–165: *Alder trees*

163

*Pages 172–173: Columbia River Gorge from Crown Point to Beacon Rock*

*Page 174: Washington State Ferry on Puget Sound*

*Page 175: Above, smelt; below, pink, or "humpie," salmon heading towards spawning beds*

Pages 176–177: *Estuary of the Khutzeymateen River, British Columbia*

Page 178: *Jewakwa Glacier, British Columbia*

Page 179: *Bute Inlet, British Columbia*

Page 180: *Summit of the Oregon Cascades, looking north*

Page 181: *Pacific coast along Tillamook Bay, Oregon*

Pages 182–183: *Mount Stuart reflecting in Lake Ingalls, Washington*

## ACKNOWLEDGMENTS

I have always felt that I was photographing for my friends, bringing home exotic wonders from my travels. Many, many people have helped me along the way as guides, companions, philosophers, and interpreters of the vision, but a few have been especially helpful. I wish to thank Barry Lopez, the Biasi family, Chip Greening, Ancil Nance, Bryan Peterson, Heidi and Robin Rickabaugh, the Clifton Street inmates, David Kelly, Martha Hill, Bill Kemsley, the Dickharts, Kate Clinton, Ed Cookman, and of course, Agatha. For help in gaining access to and interpreting parts of the landscape, I am indebted to Don Peterson and Don Swanson of the United States Geological Service, Paul George and Ken Lay of the Western Canada Wilderness Committee, Wayne McCrory, Bruce Brown, Jim Borrowman, Mike Murtha of the British Columbia Parks, Nancy Russell of Friends of the Columbia Gorge, and Jim Montieth of Oregon Natural Resources Council. Gratitude also to the staff at Rizzoli: Bill Dworkin, who suggested that I propose the book; my editor, Solveig Williams; and my designer, Gilda Hannah.

This book is a direct reflection of the powerful help, care, and love of Terry Coons, Bruce Johnston, Ann Guilfoyle, Dennis Wiancko, Joanna Priestley, my pilot, Doug Brazil; my parents, Alice and Bernard Braasch; and my beloved partner, Maryjo Anderson—for all of whom I reserve my deepest gratitude. Thanks be to God, the Great Spirit, who makes everything possible.

## NOTES ON THE PHOTOGRAPHY

My view of the work of photography has little to do with equipment and film, and everything to do with the effects of light and point of view. The awareness of light extends beyond the obvious sunsets and water reflections (wonderful though they are) to include the glimmer of frost, the glow that seems to come from within water before dawn, and the subtle gradations of leaf color in the rain forest. I tend to base my exposures on the highlights, which can lead to very dramatic underexposures and silhouettes of darker parts of the photograph (pp. 78, 92–93, and 125). In more delicate situations, the play of light on certain areas in contrast to darker ones contributes depth and form (pp. 112–113, 139, and 164–165).

As for point of view, it is crucial for me to break away from normal eye level. While shooting I am likely to be found on my belly confronting the smaller life forms with close-up lens (p. 51), or wide-angle at close focus (p. 131). I often photograph landscapes from roofs, mountaintops, or aircraft with flight altitudes ranging from a few hundred feet (top, p. 102) to over eight thousand (pp. 59 and 140–141). Other views that appear to be aerials (pp. 115, 180) are merely the result of seeking mountaintops under interesting lighting conditions.

For me, however, point of view also includes watching for symbolic relationships and specific moments or seasons. Being on the scene and waiting for the right time results in photographs such as those on pages 46–47, 54–55, 110–111, 142–143, 155, 166–167, and 168–169. In most cases I visualized and then searched for a particular picture, finally capturing it at a magic moment. There are a few happy accidents: one must always be alert, curious, and well prepared.

Part of my preparation has been to sharpen an innate sense of design, pattern, and composition. Although the subject matter is diverse, my style unifies this volume's collection with strong diagonals (pp. 150–151), pure patterns (pp. 80–81), powerful and congruent shapes (pp. 38, 148–149), and complementary colors (pp. 134–135). I often shoot late into the evening and in stormy weather. A large tripod to support my Nikon equipment during long exposures allows a greater depth of field (p. 2), or shows inherent motion (pp. 126–127). At other times I choose to isolate part of a scene, allowing other elements to be out of focus (pp. 144–145). Eleven of the photographs in this book were made on Fujichrome 50, the rest on Kodachrome 25 and 64 with Nikkor lenses ranging from 20mm to 400mm.

Gary Braasch
Nehalem, Oregon
November 1987